Park Güell

Origins

Lying to the north of the Sierra de Collserola, and marking the upper limits of the district of Gracia –a separate township until 1897, and even today a suburb with a distinctive character– there was a mountain, whose summit is Tibidabo, known as "Montaña Pelada" (the Bald Mountain) because of its scant vegetation. In those days, there were only a few big estates there, such as Can Montaner de

Aerial view of Parque Güell.

Dalt, and other smaller properties given over to farming the land. But by a series of coincidences, and within a very few years, this somewhat neglected terrain was destined to become one of the most important architectural monumental environments; a park which would, in time, achieve the title of "Monument of Humanity".

It was the idea of Don Eusebi Güell i Bacigalupi, an industrial entrepreneur and great patron of the arts, champion of all things fine and constructive and in any way able to contribute to the development of Catalonia.

Güell had spent a long time in England, and had heard that in London, 30 km out in the suburbs, also near Leicester and elsewhere in places like Letchworth and Hampstead Garden, they were building what were called "Garden Cities", known today as "housing developments". This entailed the founding of a town and the provision of all the essential services for its inhabitants, in one simultaneous operation. Güell returned to Barcelona fired with the idea of doing something similar, and even of finishing "his" garden city before the English, and so of building the first housing development in the world.

He entrusted its study and planning to the architect Antoni Gaudí, who set to work on the preparation of the mountain which Güell had bought - that is, the estate known as Can Montaner de Dalt, together with two other smaller properties.

Every ten metres there are medallions bearing the names of PARK and GÜELL alternately.

The construction began in early 1900, and was to be carried out in three phases. Although the third phase was never completed, this development was still intended to provide sixty lots for single-family houses. But the years went by, and the citizens of Barcelona did not buy them. In those days, at the beginning of this century, its position was thought to be rather isolated, and too far away from the city. And so this project, in which Güell had invested so many dreams, was considered a failure. Only three of the sixty houses planned were built: Can Montaner de Dalt which, extended and renovated, was to become the residence of its owner, Don Eusebi Güell; the house of the lawyer Trías Doménech, work of the architect Juli Batllevell;

and a third house, built to a design by Francesc Berenguer, and bought by Antoni Gaudí in 1906, who was to live there until shortly before his death in 1926. These three houses are still in existence. Today, Güell's is a school; the Trías house still belongs to the family; and the third has become a commemorative museum, the Casa-Museo Gaudí.

That, in brief, is the story of this park, constructed at the will of Eusebi Güell, and turned into a masterpiece of creative genius by his architect.

Its failure was partly due to Güell's death in 1918, shortly before the end of what was known as the European War - work on the Güell's property had already been suspended in 1914, at the onset

of that war. After the suspension of the work, some years passed before the park was finally acquired in 1922 by the Ayuntamiento of Barcelona. Between that time and the present, this creation of Gaudí has acquired an extraordinary prestige throughout the world, and Parque Güell has come to represent almost the essence of its city, so much so that a visit here is almost compulsory for anyone wishing to get to know the real Barcelona.

The entrance and the two pavilions

If we go up by Calle Larrard, the surname of a noble Barcelona family who owned these lands, we arrive at Calle de Olot, the name of a city in the Catalan Pyrenees. There we find ourselves facing a boundary wall decorated with mosaics and some large circular panels, on which is inscribed the name PARK GÜELL. (The word PARK, with its final K, shows the English origin of this word, which is used to describe a garden of certain proportions was introduced into Spain at the end of the last century, and for some years it kept its English spelling). The main entrance is right here, with a large iron gate called the Palmetto Gate –in Catalan, *margalló*– since it is made in the form of the leaves of this palm plant. This gate came from the garden wall of the Casa Vicens, in Calle de Carolinas, also in the district of Gracia. Next to this gate there are two most singular pavilions - perhaps even more fantastic than the Casa Batlló in the Paseo de Gracia, being built by Gaudi at the same time as he was engaged on the construction

Spire culminating in a four-armed cross, from the pavilion on the left going in.

Aerial view of the entrance of the Park showing both pavilions: on the left, the administration centre, and on the right, the porter's lodge.

of the Park. From here, you can already see the stairway which ascends to the Teatro Griego, also known as the Hall of the Hundred Columns, and take in at one glance the main buildings of the park.

The pavilion on the left, distinguished by its great spire crowned by a cross with four arms –a signature feature of Gaudí's work– was once the Park's Administration Office, while the pavilion on the right was the porter's lodge. The porter's flat occupied the ground floor or rather part of this floor, and there is also an upper floor and an attic. Outside, there are two verandas, and a dome topped by a red, bell-shaped dome with white details –these details are in fact small cups used at that time for drinking chocolate. The rest of the building is also clad in ceramic –*trencadís*, or small

fragments of ceramic, which completely cover the building with their colour. This very feature is one of the signatures of Gaudí's architecture –to cover his buildings with colours.

The pavilion on the left, planned as the administration of the "garden city", is almost like the Grimms Brothers' tale of Ton and Guida (Hansel and Gretel) brought to life. It too is topped by a dome covering the central part of the house. Its 16 metre high spire, decorated with coloured ceramic which gives it an undulating shape, and with chequered designs, is topped with a typical four-armed Gaudí cross.

But before beginning the climb up the central stairway, through which a fountain descends, dividing it into two, we should examine some cave-

Roof of the porter's lodge pavilion.

type structures on either side the entrance. The one on the right has a central column and was meant to accommodate carriages. That on the left forms a structure which has today become an always-lively café-bar, and which also houses the Laia Bookshop selling books and souvenirs of the park and of Gaudí's work.

The central fountain and the dragon, or iguana

The main built area of the park ascends by this double stairway as far as the so-called Teatro Griego. Here, we can see a series of stepped platforms over which cascades water from a tank filled by a spring, exploited by Güell for a time under the name of Sarba.

In the first part of the cascade that we can see, the platform over which the water trickles is made up of trunks or roots, like man-made stalactites. Looking up to the next platform, we see a medallion with the head of a snake and, behind it, the shield of Catalonia with its the four bars. Another platform, the third, follows, in the shape of the famous *Dragón del Parque Güell*, a large dragon or iguana, covered in ceramic in tones of yellow and blue. The spring water trickles from its mouth, descends to the serpent-medallion and then over the false stalactites of the first platform.

Stairway ascending to the Hall of the Hundred Columns, ›
with the Park's ceramic-coated dragon

Further up, and just below the columns, you can see and even sit on a bench protected by a concave dome where, so the story goes, the wind never blows.

The house of Conde Güell and the gardens on the right

Going up by the main stairway we see, both to our right and to our left, a wall covered with multi-coloured ceramic, with lively relief-work tiling in a host of varied patterns. This wall culminates in some Moslem-style crenallations which echo the shape of the pavilions at the entrance. On a landing in this stairway, on the left, there is the entry to a garden where a building can be seen. This is the house where Güell lived out his last years, and where he died in 1918. Previously, at the end of the nineteenth century, the house had belonged to Antonio Larrard, passing into the hands of Salvador Samà, Marqués of Marinau, in 1890, and sold nine years later to Eusebi Güell. This old house was finely renovated and remodelled by Gaudí, Jujol

The dragon or giant iguana made of "trencadís", in which the colours yellow and blue predominate.

Front view of the stairway giving access to the Sala de las Cien Columnas.

and other artists. Today, however, it has changed completely, following various adaptations, and has been in use for many years as a municipal school.

On our right, there is levelled area, of modern design and in the style of an English garden. It was here that, in 1954, the organization "Amigos de Gaudí" proposed to install sculptures by contemporary artists in a homage to Gaudí. There were only four donations, and their plan for this section of the town never became a reality.

The Hall of the Hundred Columns

The two stairways finally end below the great hypostyle room, also called the "Room of the Hundred Columns" –although in fact there are only 86. This great covered space was meant to house a daily street market to supply the needs of the inhabitants of the Garden City housing development.

Here, you will realise that you are standing under an infinity of domes, with columns between them holding up the roof. You will also notice that these columns have Greek forebears, being in a Doric style, though heavily modified. The columns on the outside perimeter are placed at an angle to neutralize the force of the roof, which is occupied by the famous bench, while those on the inside are vertical. The whole roof, between the columns, is covered with spherical domes lined with mosaic or white *trencadís*. One of the unusual elements to

Seat protected from the wind, at the top of the main stairway.

Hexagons set into the wall, with ceramic which calls to mind Moslem originals.

note are the false vault key-stones, whose purpose is purely decorative. Here, their creator, Josep Mª Jujol, achieved one of his most interesting works, and one of unprecedented artistic value. In fact, these key-stones are really collages, made from pieces of waste material from ceramic kilns; you can see plates, mirrors, and broken bottles, placed by the artist on this magic roof of the great hall.

Fountain with dragon's head and the shield of Catalonia.

Colonnade of the hall under the great square.

Colonnade of the so-called Teatro Griego or Hall of the Hundred Columns.

You can also discover, among the other objects, porcelain cups, objects of everyday use, and even a broken doll found by Jujol; all this is extremely audacious, bearing in mind the era in which these roof panels were constructed.

These false keystones, as well as the small domes covered with white ceramic and the bases of the columns, are all masterpieces of modern art. You will also see some iron hooks still in place, once used to hold the lamps which lit the great hall at night. The illumination at the foot of each column is of recent installation.

The great central square

Climbing the stair on our right, we reach a square, whose surface lies over part of the room below, and which extends as far as the garden and woods which go on up to the summit of the mountain. This square, together with the open market below, was destined to be the centre of life for the inhabitants of the park. Although it never achieved this purpose, from the time it was completed and up to the present day, this space has always been a centre for visitors to the park. It has been used as a

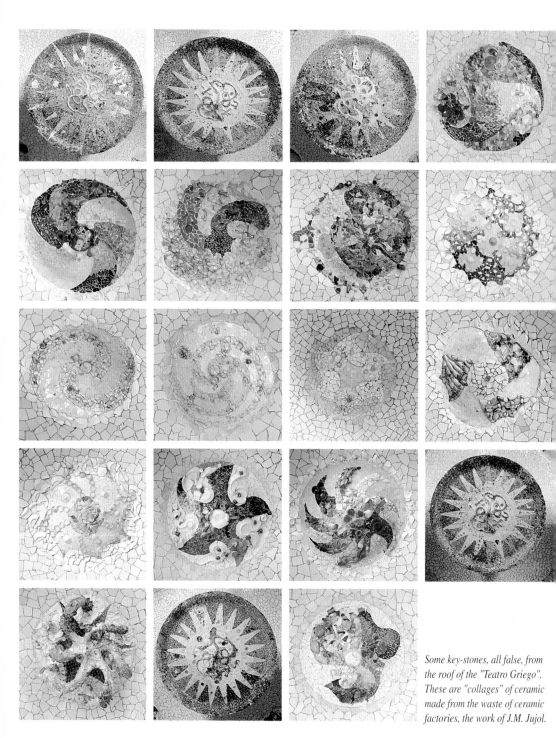

Some key-stones, all false, from the roof of the "Teatro Griego". These are "collages" of ceramic made from the waste of ceramic factories, the work of J.M. Jujol.

12

venue for large public gatherings such as the anniversary celebrations of organizations, or all kinds of events run by social, political and even religious entities. To give only one example, one of the biggest events was the speech given by Salvador Dalí on the night of 29th September 1956, organized by the body "Amigos de Gaudí", a quite unique occasion. The theme of his speech was Gaudí.

This centre of the park, which was to have been the focus of the garden city, has one exceptional feature which has impressed artists all over the world: the bench which runs round the southern perimeter of the square.

The serpentine bench

Called the serpentine bench because of its winding shape, not a gratuitous feature, but a practical one dictated by the disposition of the columns holding up the roof of the hall below. But its main interest lies in the ceramic work which covers it, one of the keys of its originality and its value as a work of art. As one of Gaudí's most loyal collaborators, the sculptor Josep Matamala, tells us, Gaudí had requested an estimate for this work from a company in Valencia with a long tradition in what was in effect not only a craft, but also an art. But

The outer part of the serpentine bench which bounds the main square.

An example of a decorative element, treated with relief work and "movement".

A detail of the bench, with fragmented ceramic decoration, or "trencadís".

a general strike affecting the sector including the kilns involved in this type of work lasted for some months and, when it finished, the estimate for the job had increased so much that it was decided to look to other workshops. But Gaudí had the splendid idea for solving the problem: this meant going to the local ceramic kilns making prefabricated pieces, and using these pieces to make the *trencadís*. So they bought carts (in these days there were no vans), and filled them with ceramic waste and broken crockery to be found in the waste heaps attached to the workshops. Using this, and the waste material from several kilns, this marvellous work was brought into being –a work which foreshadows and brings together the concepts of contemporary painting. So not only was the end result quite splendid, but it was achieved with a minimum cost in materials.

Mention must made here of Josep Maria Jujol, the creator of the coloured ceramic work of the park –a great artist, and a real creative spirit ahead of his time, for whom Gaudí had a great admiration and in whom he had absolute confidence. Jujol used an original strategy, sometimes leaving the site workers to choose ceramic fragments from the stored heaps, and position them in the mortar. Sometimes Jujol would re-do their work, but on other occasions he would tell them: "Very good! Magnificent!" And so their work was kept, and the men who had done it felt that they too were creators and artists, rather like Jujol and Gaudí themselves.

This then is the serpentine bench –a comfortable seat in spite of its hard surface– made from the

Perspective of the bench in the main square of the Park. ❯

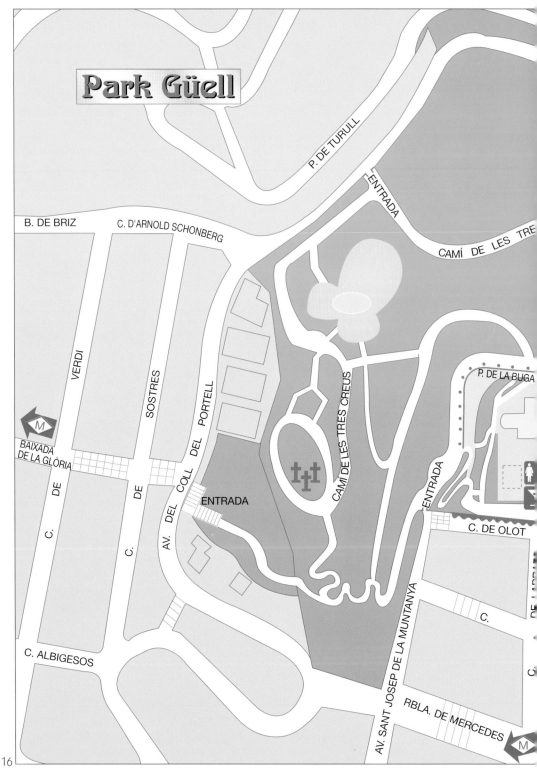

Park Güell

P. DE TURULL

ENTRADA

CAMÍ DE LES TRE

B. DE BRIZ

C. D'ARNOLD SCHONBERG

P. DE LA BUGA

VERDI

SOSTRES

AV. DEL COLL DEL PORTELL

CAMÍ DE LES TRES CREUS

BAIXADA DE LA GLÒRIA

C. DE

C. DE

ENTRADA

ENTRADA

C. DE OLOT

C.

DE L'ABR

C. ALBIGESOS

AV. SANT JOSEP DE LA MUNTANYA

C.

RBLA. DE MERCEDES

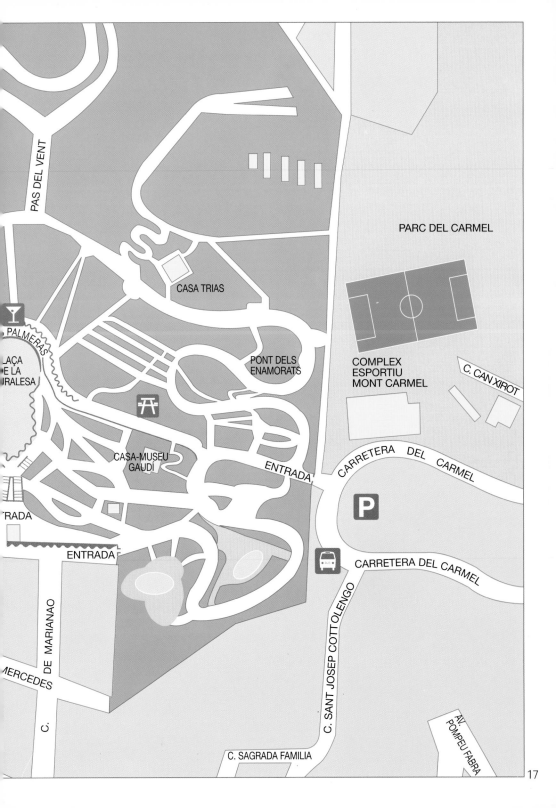

PAS DEL VENT

PARC DEL CARMEL

CASA TRIAS

PALMERAS

LAÇA
E LA
URALESA

PONT DELS
ENAMORATS

COMPLEX
ESPORTIU
MONT CARMEL

C. CAN XIROT

CASA-MUSEU
GAUDÍ

ENTRADA

CARRETERA DEL CARMEL

RADA

P

ENTRADA

CARRETERA DEL CARMEL

DE MARIANAO

MERCEDES

C. SANT JOSEP COTTOLENGO

C.

C. SAGRADA FAMILIA

AV. POMPEU FABRA

A porticoed passage with leaning columns to counterbalance the slope. ⟩

Figure known as "la bugadera" (the washerwoman), a kind of caryatid in the porticoes next to the square and facing the house of Conde Güell, now a school.

most trivial and everyday waste whose broken, dismembered and fragmented elements have been transformed into one of the great works in the history of the twentieth century art.

The porticoes, covered ways of the Parque Güell

Looking northwards before leaving the square, and with the city at our back, we can see a wall topped by a series of large planters in the shape of palm trees, whose purpose is to establish a harmony with nature, between the palm trees planted in front of the wall and their constructed equivalents, which follow the rhythm of the neighbouring trees.

And then, going down a few steps on the other side, as if we were returning to the hall of the columns, we find one of the Park's porticoes. These structures were planned by Gaudí not only to take advantage of the buttresses holding up the higher levels of ground but also to provide covered ways running round the whole park, protecting its inhabitants or their visitors from the sun and the rain in their walks through the park.

They consist of four covered passages not actually linked, although the architect had planned that they should form one uninterrupted passage.

The portico behind Güell's house –which we visit after our tour of the square and its multi-coloured serpentine bench– seen in perspective, takes the shape of a sea wave, with the inclination of its columns serving to counterbalance the slope above, and its wall maintaining the curvature and the sloping line of the columns. For this reason, what was in essence a banking became a tunnel. In other words, with this one boundary feature, it manages to accomplish two important functions: to counterbalance the pressure at its edge, and to use its cavity for the movement and use of its visitors.

After this covered passage, which you can follow right to the end to admire its leaning, twisted columns, and the various figures which adorn them, you must either go back to the square or else ascend by the path above. This path takes us to the right hand side of the park, to where the building which today houses the Casa-Museo Gaudí is situated. From here, following the avenue which starts at the Carretera del Carmelo, we climb to the so-called *Pont de Dalt*, which is another covered passageway, although totally different from the one we have

Another pedestrianized passage, above which runs the road which goes round the Park.

already seen, and where a brutally distorted "carob tree" construction can be seen, in tune with Gaudí's precept that the work of man should be confused with the work of nature.

Following the viaduct to arrive at the highest point, known as "Les Tres Creus"

Climbing on up, by what is today a surfaced path, some stone benches hang in empty space from one of these passageways. Between them, there are some tall planters, supported by the columns which are topped by agave plants. These are the origin of the rumour in Europe that Gaudí built trees out of stone.

Continue up to the summit of Montaña Pelada, where Güell had intended to build a chapel. In the

end, a small stone mound was built, with three crosses, which explain its name "Les Tres Creus". From here you can admire a view of the city totally different from the usual ones, such as those from Tibidabo or Montjüic.

On the way down, it is almost obligatory, and also a suitable homage to the creator of this original landscaped mountain, to visit the Casa-Museo Gaudí, where the architect lived from 1906 to 1926. He left the house to go to live in the Temple of the Sagrada Familia eight months before his death, the story of which is common knowledge –that he suffered a traffic accident, and was knocked down by a tram. He first lived here with some relatives and later alone. Every working day, at eight in the morning, he would leave to go to his building sites, and especially the one he loved most, his Temple,

Porticoed walkway.

The viaduct flanked by stone planters.

returning at nightfall. This return journey he made on foot, in conformance with his idea that human beings should walk ten kilometres every day, the distance from the Park to the temple, to San Felipe Neri (next to the Cathedral) and back again to the Park.

A covered passageway next to the villa of the Casa-Museo Gaudí.

Construction of the front portico, where the stones give the sensation of coming loose and flying away.

The Casa-Museo Gaudí

This villa, which was built for the works manager, José Pardo, and commissioned from Francesc Berenguer, one of the most faithful of Gaudí's collaborators. This house was built with aim of enticing some future tenants for the Garden City. It was completed in 1905, and was bought by Antoní Gaudí, who had to take out a mortgage to do so, since he did not have sufficient funds to buy it outright.

Gaudí lived there from 1906 to 1926, leaving it shortly before his death, it passed by inheritance to the Works Committee of the Sagrada Familia.

The house is Modernist in style, although with clear signs of Berenguer's personality, and with some influences from Gaudí.

We go in through the door form the walkway which begins in the great square of the park and ends where it meets the Carretera del Carmelo. Here, there is a large parking lot and the bus stop for the number 24 and 25 buses and it is through this entry that the majority of the coaches carrying school and tourist groups, and private cars, enter the Park. We go down to the house, which lies on a lower level, and the first thing we see is the garden, typifying Gaudí's taste, and his belief it should contain local plants and not need much maintenance. A veritable explosion of metalwork designed by Gaudí can also be seen there: as a centre-piece, the cross, an original work coming from the roof of the Miralles house in the Paseo Manuel Girona in Barcelona. On the wall, there is a series of mosaic medallions, from the same series as those which can be seen in the park, giving a very Gaudí-style feel to this part of the garden. Another outstanding element of the garden, making it such a unique space, is the Paseo de Circunvalación, with its iron parabolic arches, designed by Gaudí. and which illustrates one of his preoccupations, and which are fully worked out

in what is today called the "Espai Gaudí", in the Pedrera building. Here this totally enclosing structure, in this case enclosing a garden instead of a building, is in the form of a delightful pergola, whose construction dates from the same years as the Casa Milá, around 1908-1909.

Contents of the Casa-Museo Gaudí

On entering the house, we see in the hall a bronze bust of Antoni Gaudí i Cornet (1852-1926), the only portrait carried out from life, and the work of the sculptor J. Matamala Flotats, the most faithful of

Porch through which runs the path round the Park.

The Casa-Museo Gaudí.

*Villa built by the architect Francesc Berenguer. Bought by
Gaudí, who lived there from 1906 to 1926, the year of his
death. Today houses the museum dedicated to the architect.*

Gaudí's collaborators. The first room past the
souvenir and publications shop is that known as
the Casa Calvet, in which furniture from this house
in Calle Caspe, 48, in Barcelona, is exhibited.
Going along a corridor we arrive at the dining room,
where there is some famous furniture belonging to
the Batlló family, from their house in Paseo de
Gracia, 43. Here we can see the chair which was a
prototype of anatomical design. We can also see,
on our right, the *Salón Calvet*, made to a design of
Gaudí, one of whose armchairs was used as the
seat for the Holy Father when he visited the Temple
of the Sagrada Familia, in 1980. And on the far
side of the dining room table, there is a room with
furniture left by the Italian Chiappo-Arietti family,

who lived in the house from 1927 to 1960, the
year when it ceased being the property of the
Amigos de Gaudí and became a commemorative
museum dedicated to its architect.

If we climb to the first floor, we will see a bust
of Eusebio Güell (1846-1918), the work of the
sculptor brothers Oslé, and another portrait of
Gaudí's patron, the work of the painter Julio
Moisés, as well as the chairs known as "de los gatos
y ratones" (of cats and mice). There are also
drawings by Josep Mª Jujol (1879-1949), Gaudí's
collaborator and one of the great artists of the
twentieth century. In the Gallery are kept all that
remains on the Temple of the Sagrada Familia: the
model of a column - a work which on its own gives

witness to the genius of an artist, as a new form in the history of art; the sketch of the sculptor Jaume Busquets for the sculptural group on the façade of the Nacimiento in the Temple; and the maquette of the schools of the Sagrada Familia, one of the great architectural inventions of Gaudí.

Continuing, we find the Sala Ibarz-Marco, with furniture of the most pronounced *Art nouveau* or

Casa-Museo Gaudí: dining-room with furniture from the Casa Batlló, designed by Gaudí.

⟨ *Bronze bust of Antoni Gaudí, work of Josep Matamala Flotats.*

Bedroom with Gaudí's bed.

Casa-Museo Gaudí: The Sala Ibarz-Marco, with furniture designed by A. Clapés and A. Gaudí. 〉

typically Modernist style, designed by the artist, painter and collaborator of Gaudí, Aleix Clapés (1850-1920), with collaboration from the master himself. In the next room there is furniture from the Casa Milá, and also paving from this house (the same as that found on the Paseo de Gracia). Another room is Gaudí's studio, with sculptures by his collaborators, the desk of the architect Vilaseca, a contemporary of Gaudí, and some original Gaudí drawings. The last room is his bedroom, with the actual Modernist-style iron bedstead which Gaudí used, a cross by the sculptor Carles Mani, and the death mask of the artist, work of the sculptor Matamala.

From 1998 it will be possible to visit the third floor, where you can find the Sala Mani, with works by the sculptor Carles Mani (1866-1911), one of Gaudí's collaborators, a painting by Francesc Gimeno and a drawing by Picasso.

This floor also houses an extensive collection (more than thirty thousand) of catalogues from art exhibitions, which form part of the library's

Casa-Museo Gaudí: Gaudí's office.

collection. And last of all, from the terrace, you can obtain fine views over the Park and Barcelona. Observe here two chimney-stacks covered in *trencadís*, key but little-known examples of Gaudí's genius, which influenced some works of Joan Miró.

It should be added that the library, and a video facility, will be inaugurated before the end of the year 1999. The way out is back through to the main door, or if you wish, you can leave by the door at the bottom of the garden, and go through the "Pont de Baix", porticoed passage, whose construction differs yet again from the porticoes already seen.

A stone staircase will take you to the exit on the Carretera del Carmelo, and out of the park. The cast-iron door shaped to imitate the stones on the wall, which closes behind the park, is a recent addition.

Central salon of the Casa-Museo Gaudí, with furniture designed by A. Clapés and A. Gaudí, the portrait of Eusebi Güell by Julio Moisés, and the "de los gatos y ratones" chairs created by Gaudí.

BARCELONA GAUDÍ

1. FANALS PL. REIAL (1878-1879)
2. CASA VICENS (1878-1885)
3. FINCA GÜELL (1884-1887)
4. TERESINES (1888-1889)
5. PALAU GÜELL (1886-1891)
6. SAGRADA FAMÍLIA (1884-1926)
7. BELLESGUARD (1900-1902)
8. CASA CALVET (1898-1904)
9. CASA BATLLÓ (1904-1906)
10. PARC GÜELL (1900-1914)
11. CASA MILÀ (1906-1910)
12. COLÒNIA GÜELL (1890-1915)